HAPPY BIRTHDAY

TO

....

WITH LOVE FROM

....

And Bob

HAPPY BIRTHDAY—LOVE . . .
Complete Series

Jane Austen

Joan Crawford

Bette Davis

Liam Gallagher

Audrey Hepburn

John Lennon

Bob Marley

Marilyn Monroe

Michelle Obama

Jackie Kennedy Onassis

Elvis Presley

Keith Richards

Frank Sinatra

Elizabeth Taylor

Oscar Wilde

HAPPY BIRTHDAY
Love, Bob

ON YOUR SPECIAL DAY

ENJOY THE WIT AND WISDOM OF

BOB MARLEY

THE KING OF REGGAE

Edited by Jade Riley

CELEBRATION BOOKS

THIS IS A CELEBRATION BOOK

Published by Celebration Books 2023
Celebration Books is an imprint of Dean Street Press

Text & Design Copyright © 2023 Celebration Books

All Rights Reserved. No part of this publication may be reproduced, stored in or transmitted in any form or by any means without the written permission of the copyright owner and the publisher of this book.

Cover by DSP

ISBN 978 1 915393 64 7

www.deanstreetpress.co.uk

HAPPY BIRTHDAY—LOVE, BOB

The supreme Bob Marley started the journey of life on his grandfather's farm in St. Ann parish—the son of an English father and a Jamaican mother. At the age of twelve, he found his way to ska music, the precursor of reggae, after moving to the city of Kingston. Later, with Peter Tosh and Bunny Wailer, he formed the first version of the Wailers, and the 1960s and '70s saw the group put out albums, break up, and reform with new members, all while perfecting their music, and creating indelible anthems of love, spirituality and revolution. During this time, Bob also began his journey into the Rastafarian faith, a religion which regards King Selassie of Ethiopia as the Messiah—he is said to be the 225th descendant of King Solomon and the Queen of Sheba. There can be no doubt that the religion had a monumental influence on Bob Marley and his message of peace, conveyed through songs of love and freedom.

As a mature artist, Bob Marley used his power and success to help the oppressed everywhere, especially in Africa. He even managed to get two political opponents to come on stage and shake hands at the Smile Jamaica concert of 1976. Politics aside, one of Bob's biggest loves was the game of soccer, telling one journalist: "If you want to get to know me, you will have to play football against me and the Wailers." Sadly, the globally loved icon left us in 1981. He is honored widely; from a statue erected in Serbia to Bob Marley Boulevard in Brooklyn, New York. He is considered a prophet by the Hopi native American people, and revered throughout India. It seems the entire world is willing to get up and stand up for Bob Marley.

Bob Marley

True friends are like stars; you can only recognize them when it's dark around you.

One good thing about music—
when it hits you,
you feel no pain.

My music will go on forever. Maybe it's a fool say that, but when me know facts, me can say facts.

Every man got the right to decide his own destiny.

Man is a universe within himself.

Some people are so poor all they have is money.

If she's amazing, she won't be easy. If she's easy, she won't be amazing. If she's worth it, you won't give up. If you give up, you're not worthy. Truth is, everybody is going to hurt you; you just gotta find the ones worth suffering for.

"Money is numbers, and numbers never end. If it takes money to be happy, your search for happiness will never end."

In the abundance of water, a fool is thirsty.

In this bright future, you can't forget your past.

"I have a BMW. But only because BMW stands for Bob Marley and The Wailers, and not because I need an expensive car.

Live for yourself, and you will live in vain. Live for others, and you will live again.

Only once in your life,
I truly believe, you
find someone who
can completely turn
your world around.

Make way for the positive day.

Judge not, before you judge yourself. Judge not, if you're not ready for judgment.

When the root is strong, the fruit is sweet.

"I know that I'm not perfect and that I don't claim to be. So before you point your fingers, make sure your hands are clean.

If something can corrupt you, you're corrupt already.

"Don't complicate your mind.

Money can't buy life.

Some will hate you, pretend they love you, now then behind they try to eliminate you.

Man can't do without God. Just like you're thirsty, you have to drink water. You just can't go without God.

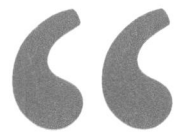

The people who were trying to make this world worse are not taking the day off. Why should I?

My life is only important if I can help plenty of people.

Free speech carries with it some freedom to listen.

Better to die fighting for freedom than be a prisoner all the days of your life.

I have no have education. I have inspiration. If I was educated, I would be a damn fool.

Everything is political. I will never be a politician or even think political. Me just deal with life and nature. That is the greatest thing to me.

Today, people struggle to find what's real. Everything has become so synthetic that a lot of people, all they want is to grasp onto hope.

Life and Jah are one in the same. Jah is the gift of existence. I am in some way eternal; I will never be duplicated. The singularity of every man and woman is Jah's gift. What we struggle to make of it is our sole gift to Jah. The process of what that struggle becomes, in time, the Truth.

Me only have one ambition, y'know. I only have one thing I really like to see happen. I like to see mankind live together— black, white, Chinese, everyone—that's all.

"Rasta not a culture; it's a reality."

The greatness of a man is not in how much wealth he acquires. It is in his integrity and his ability to affect those around him positively.

A hungry mob is an angry mob.

"Wake up and live."

The more people smoke herb, the more Babylon fall.

Just because you are happy, it does not mean that the day is perfect but that you have looked beyond its imperfections.

Light up the darkness.

We know where we're going 'cause we know where we're from.

Nothing is wrong if it makes you happy.

Love hard when there is love to be had.

Herb is the healing of a nation, alcohol is the destruction.

Football is a part of I. When I play, the world wakes up around me.

You entertain people who are satisfied. Hungry people can't be entertained—or people who are afraid. You can't entertain a man who has no food.

Bob Marley isn't my name. I don't even know my name yet.

"The most beautiful things are not perfect. They are special.

"

The most beautiful curve on a woman's body is her smile.

You can't find the right roads when the streets are paved.

None but ourselves can free our minds.

A foolish dog barks at a flying bird.

It's the music.
Your heart
is in your
ears.

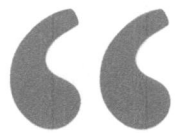

"Politics and church are the same. They keep the people in ignorance.

"

Football is freedom, a whole universe.

There's a natural mystic blowing through the air. If you listen carefully now, you will hear.

Every man gotta right to decide his own destiny.

"Stop and think a little: Are you the victim of the system?

"My fear is my only courage."

"If you know your history, then you would know where you coming from, then you wouldn't have to ask me, who the heck do I think I am?

The good times of today are the sad thoughts of tomorrow.

You never know how strong you are until being strong is the only choice you have.

The biggest coward
of a man is to awaken
the love of a woman
without the intention
of loving her.

Why drink and drive if I can smoke and fly?

The winds that sometimes take something we love are the same that bring us something we learn to love. Therefore we should not cry about something that was taken from us, but, yes, love what we have been given. Because what is really ours is never gone forever.

You may not be her first, her last, or her only. She loved before she may love again. But if she loves you now, what else matters?

When one door is closed, don't you know that many more are open?

The beauty of love.
The love of beauty.

The greener you are, the wiser you will be.

Overcome the devils with a thing called love.

Sometimes you have to fight with music.

My favorite herb—lamb's bread. Kali. I like Hawaiian. But for some reason, you communicate better with Jamaican herb. The best Jamaican herb, it have more energy, more everything to it.

If you don't start somewhere, you're gonna go nowhere.

God created people in technicolor. God has never made a difference between black, white, blue, green or pink.

My music fights against the system that teaches to live and die.

Me can't be prejudice. Me can't me no think of life that way. Because, me figure if you prejudice, that mean you have a hate. If you have a hate inside of you, you can't be righteous.

We Jah people can make it work.

Me don't dip on nobody's side. Me don't dip on the black man's side, not the white man's side. Me dip on God's side, the one who create me and cause me to come from black and white.

Have pity on those whose chances grow thinner, there ain't no hiding place from the Father of Creation.

"I don't believe in death, neither in flesh nor in spirit.

The day you stop racing is the day you win the race.

"Don't hurt her, don't change her, don't analyze and don't expect more than she can give. Smile when she makes you happy, let her know when she makes you mad, and miss her when she's not there."

Perfect guys don't exist, but there's always one guy that is perfect for you.

Some people feel the rain. Others just get wet.

> You say you love rain, but you use an umbrella to walk under it. You say you love sun, but you seek shelter when it is shining. You say you love wind, but when it comes you close your windows. So that's why I'm scared when you say you love me.

Beginnings are usually scary, and endings are usually sad, but its everything in between that makes it all worth living.

"If you get down and you quarrel everyday, you're saying praises to the devil, I say.

Don't worry about a thing 'cause every little thing gonna be all right.

B.B. Marley

ABOUT THE EDITOR

Jade Riley is a writer whose interests include old movies, art history, vintage fashion and books, books, books.

Her dream is to move to London, to write like Virginia Woolf, and to meet a man like Mr. Darcy, who owns a vacation home in Greece.

www.ingramcontent.com/pod-product-compliance
Lightning Source LLC
Chambersburg PA
CBHW021131130526
44590CB00055B/355